MACHINES AT WORK

On the Rails

IAN GRAHAM

QED Publishing

Copyright © QED Publishing 2006

First published in the UK in 2006 by
QED Publishing
A Quarto Group company
226 City Road
London EC1V 2TT
www.qed-publishing.co.uk

A catalogue record for this book is available from the British Library.

ISBN 978 1 84538 585 9

Written by Ian Graham
Produced by Calcium
Editor Sarah Medina
Foldout illustration by Ian Naylor
Picture Researcher Maria Joannou

Publisher Steve Evans
Creative Director Zeta Davies
Senior Editor Hannah Ray

Printed and bound in China

Picture credits
Key: T = top, B = bottom, C = centre, L = left, R = right, FC = front cover

Alstom 6–7, 9T, 20T, 21T; **Angel Trains** 5; **Barco** 23B; **Bombardier Transport**
6, 7, 17, 24, 27, 28–29; **Corbis**/Richard Cummins 14–15, /Colin Garratt/Milepost 92 22–23, /Noah K. Murray/Star Ledger 33,
Yuriko Nakao/Reuters 31, /Nogues Alain 23T /Neil Rabinowitz 29B, Russ Schleipman 13B, Sygma 9B, Hans Weißer 30–31,
Adam Woolfitt 15B, Michael S. Yamashita 10; **Dusseldorf Airport**/Andreas Wiese 29T; **Freightliner** 12–13, 13T; **Getty
Images**/AFP 16–21 /Photographers Choice 32–33, Reportage 8-9, Stone 20B; **Morguefile** 15T;
NASA/Bill Ingalls 11; **Photos.com** 4; **Rail Europe** 21B; **Rex Features** 26; **The Russia Experience**/
Trans Siberian Express 10-11; **With thanks to** Joe Osciak 4–5 /Joseph Tischner 24–25

Words in **bold** can be found in the Glossary on page 34.

CONTENTS

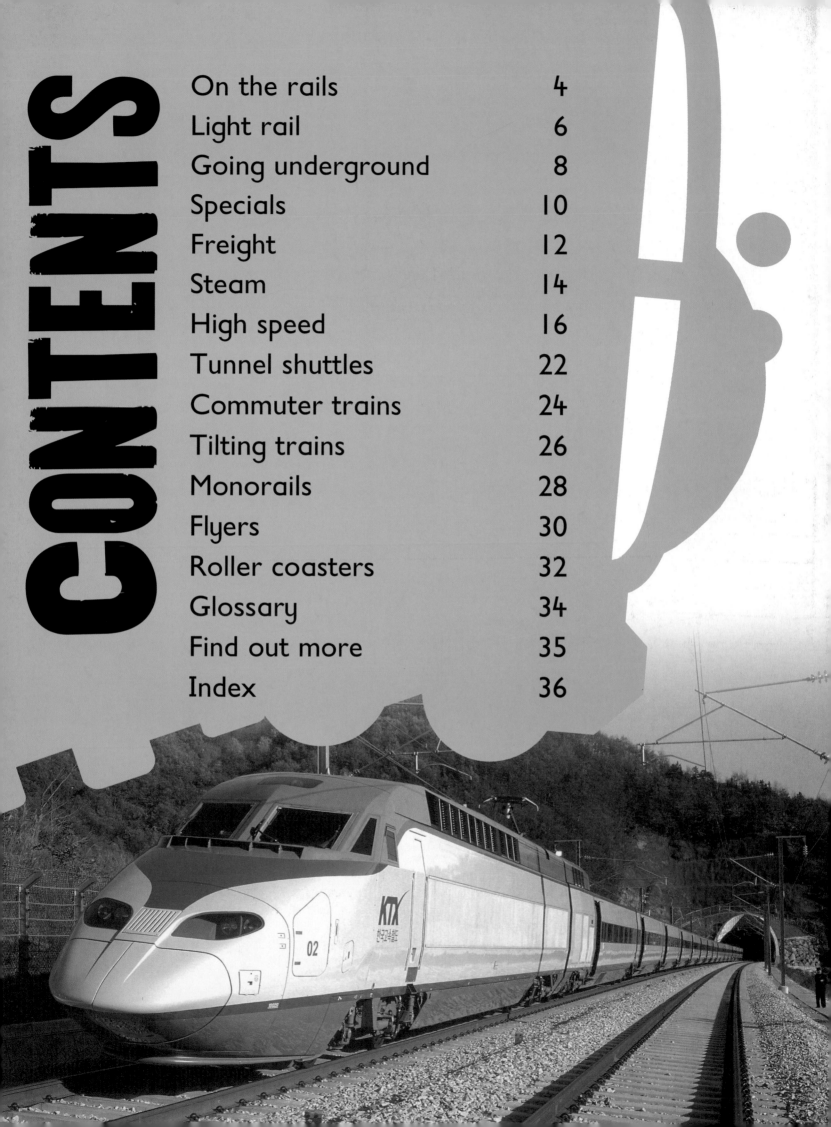

On the rails   4

Light rail   6

Going underground   8

Specials   10

Freight   12

Steam   14

High speed   16

Tunnel shuttles   22

Commuter trains   24

Tilting trains   26

Monorails   28

Flyers   30

Roller coasters   32

Glossary   34

Find out more   35

Index   36

ON THE RAILS

Railway lines crisscross the world. They spread out from major cities like huge steel spider webs. Every day, trains thunder along the tracks, carrying millions of workers into towns and cities. They take people away on holiday, and move **billions** of tonnes of goods and materials. The latest **high-speed** passenger trains carry hundreds of people in comfortable **carriages**. These trains are almost as fast as a small aeroplane. The trains that do all these jobs are very powerful machines.

▲ One train can carry as many people as hundreds of cars.

Rail or road?

Railways are a good way to move people and materials. A modern high-speed railway line can carry more traffic than a six-lane motorway, but takes up much less space. Trains create far less **air pollution** than a motorway full of traffic, so they are also kinder to the **environment**.

MOVING MOUNTAINS

Freight **trains transport the goods and materials that modern life depends on. They move mountains of gravel, earth and rock, and transport cars and other goods made in factories. They also move oil and other fuels needed to run all sorts of vehicles and machines, and deliver coal to power stations to provide the electricity we need.**

▲ Two freight trains pull **wagons** full of coal through Wyoming, USA.

2000

Amtrak

FACT!
The world's first railway locomotive was built by Richard Trevithick in 1804.

▲ After planes, high-speed passenger train is the fastest way to travel!

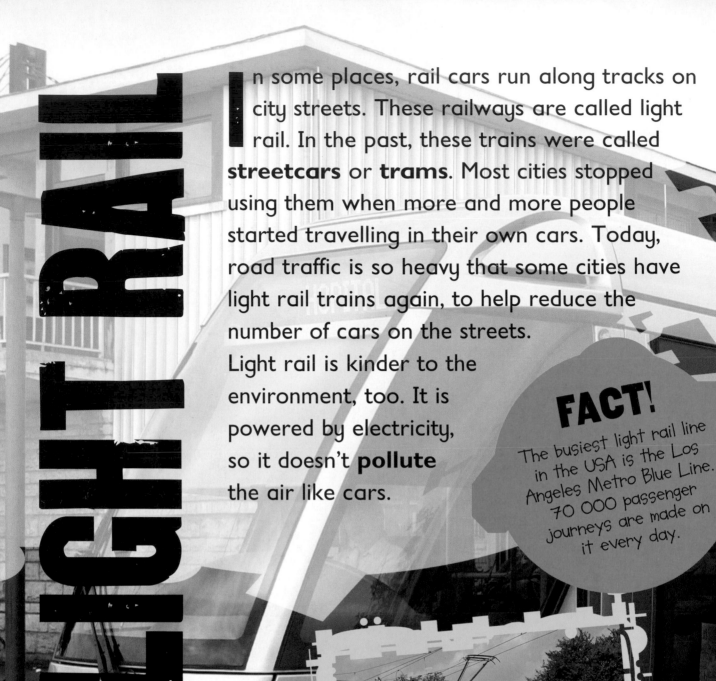

LIGHT RAIL

In some places, rail cars run along tracks on city streets. These railways are called light rail. In the past, these trains were called **streetcars** or **trams**. Most cities stopped using them when more and more people started travelling in their own cars. Today, road traffic is so heavy that some cities have light rail trains again, to help reduce the number of cars on the streets. Light rail is kinder to the environment, too. It is powered by electricity, so it doesn't **pollute** the air like cars.

FACT!

The busiest light rail line in the USA is the Los Angeles Metro Blue Line. 70 000 passenger journeys are made on it every day.

Powering up

Most light rail cars pick up the electric current they need from wires hanging over the road. A frame on top of the rail cars pushes up against the wires. As the rail cars move, the frame slides along the wires. The electric current then flows down through the frame into the vehicle's electric motors.

▲ Light rail cars can be powered from cables above the car or by an electric rail in the road.

▼ About 45 000 people a day travel on the light rail line in Orléans, in France.

JULES VERNE

54

Pédaler

Associés pour votre mobilité
unireso
Evoluons ensemble

BENDY CARS

Light rail cars have to run along existing streets, travelling alongside all the other traffic. The longer a light rail train is, the more passengers it can carry, but if it is too long, it cannot make sharp turns. The solution is to make a light rail train that bends in the middle!

▲ Light rail trains bend where the carriages connect to each other.

7

GOING UNDERGROUND

Underground railways avoid the traffic on busy city streets because the trains travel in tunnels dug under the city. Petrol or **diesel engines** would fill the stations with dangerous **fumes**, so trains that run underground are powered by electric motors. Underground railways are also called **subways** or **metros**. Some cities have fast city transport systems called **mass transit** or **rapid transit** systems. These often use underground railways, as well as railways on or even high above the ground.

➤ The New York City Subway uses enough electric power to provide light for a city of nearly 300 000 people.

▲ Line 14 in the Paris Metro has automatic trains that run without drivers.

Trains without drivers

The most modern underground railways have automatic trains — there are no drivers! The trains automatically stay a safe distance from the train in front and constantly report where they are to a control room. In France, one of the Paris Metro's lines is fully automatic. In Singapore, they are building the world's biggest automatic underground railway.

SUPER SUBWAY

The New York City Subway is the biggest underground railway in the world. When it opened in 1904, there were 28 stations. Today, there are 468! More than 6000 cars run on the Subway network. They are powered by electricity from a third rail running alongside the tracks.

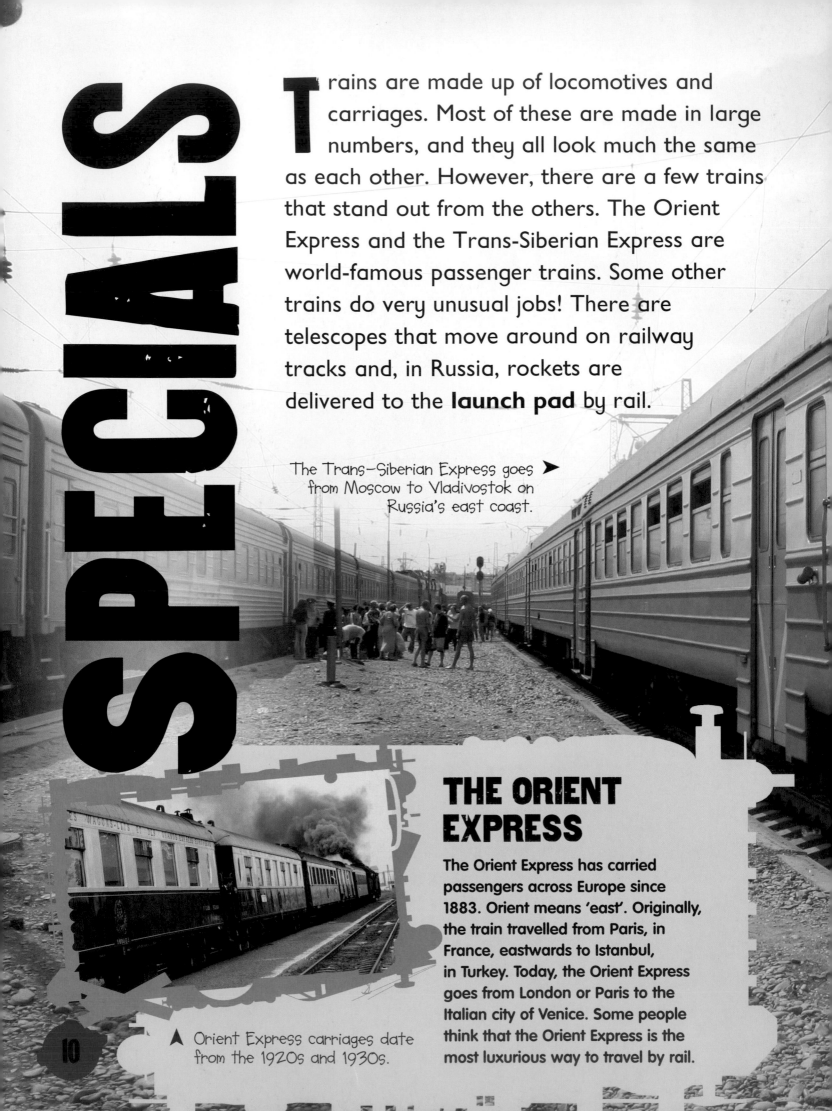

SPECIALS

Trains are made up of locomotives and carriages. Most of these are made in large numbers, and they all look much the same as each other. However, there are a few trains that stand out from the others. The Orient Express and the Trans-Siberian Express are world-famous passenger trains. Some other trains do very unusual jobs! There are telescopes that move around on railway tracks and, in Russia, rockets are delivered to the **launch pad** by rail.

The Trans-Siberian Express goes ➤ from Moscow to Vladivostok on Russia's east coast.

▲ Orient Express carriages date from the 1920s and 1930s.

THE ORIENT EXPRESS

The Orient Express has carried passengers across Europe since 1883. Orient means 'east'. Originally, the train travelled from Paris, in France, eastwards to Istanbul, in Turkey. Today, the Orient Express goes from London or Paris to the Italian city of Venice. Some people think that the Orient Express is the most luxurious way to travel by rail.

A Soyuz rocket arrives at its ➤
Russian launch pad by rail.

Rocket rail

Rocket parts arrive at the Baikonur Cosmodrome (space centre) in Russia by air. Then they are loaded onto wagons on a track beside the runway. The track leads to the building where the rockets are built. Each completed rocket is loaded onto a rail car so it can be taken out to the launch pad.

FACT!

The Trans-Siberian Express takes about seven days to complete its 9290km journey.

FREIGHT

Enormous amounts of goods and materials, known as freight, are sent by rail. In the USA, more than 1.8 billion tonnes of freight cross the country by rail every year. The heaviest freight trains carry coal away from mines in wagons. The wagons are pulled by very powerful locomotives. Three, four or even more locomotives are often hooked together to pull freight trains that have over a hundred wagons.

diesel locomotive

FACT!
The heaviest freight train weighed 99 732 tonnes. It was more than 7.3km long!

➤ Rail is the best way to carry heavy materials over long distances.

Container freight

Many goods are transported in metal boxes that are all the same size. They are called freight or shipping containers. They can be lifted off a truck and lowered onto a wagon very quickly by specially built cranes. The cranes themselves often move on rails, too.

▲ Freight containers make it quicker to load and unload freight trains.

◄ Satellites keep track of freight trains in remote parts of North America, South Africa and Australia.

freight wagon

KEEPING TRACK

For safety reasons, freight managers like to know exactly where freight is during its journey. Freight trains often have electronic boxes called transponders. They send information to receivers beside the track. The receivers then send the information on to the freight managers. Satellites track trains in remote areas. Satellite tracking does not need any equipment beside the rail line.

STEAM

The first trains were powered by steam engines. In most places, steam trains disappeared long ago. They were replaced by diesel and electric trains. Old steam trains are still used in a few places. In parts of China, India, Africa and South America, steam trains haul coal, wood and other raw materials. Some steam trains have been **restored** so that people can ride in them today.

FACT!
The world speed record for steam trains is 201kph. The record was set by a steam train called Mallard on 3 July 1938.

▲ You can see old steam trains on display at museums and history parks, like this one in Yuma in Arizona, USA.

Steam power

A steam train works by burning coal or wood to heat water. When the water gets very hot, it changes into steam. Steam takes up more space than water. The force of the steam **expanding** in a small space pushes **pistons** in and out of **cylinders**. The powerful movements of these pistons turn the train's wheels.

▲ The power to move a huge steam train comes from hot water!

▼ A miniature steam train may be small, but it is still powerful enough to pull a long line of passenger carriages.

driver's **cab**

2521

TINY TRAINS

In some places, you can go for a ride in a steam train that is much smaller than an ordinary train. Some of these miniature trains are so small that the driver has to sit on top! Even so, they work just like full-size steam trains.

power cable
supplies 25 000 volts of electricity to the train

▼ The TGV runs at full speed on its special railway lines. It can also run on ordinary lines at a lower speed.

main transformer
Changes 25 000 volts from the power cable into 1 500 volts

power car
pulls the train, with another power car at the back

FACT!
A TGV train set a world speed record for passenger trains of 515kph on a test run in 1990.

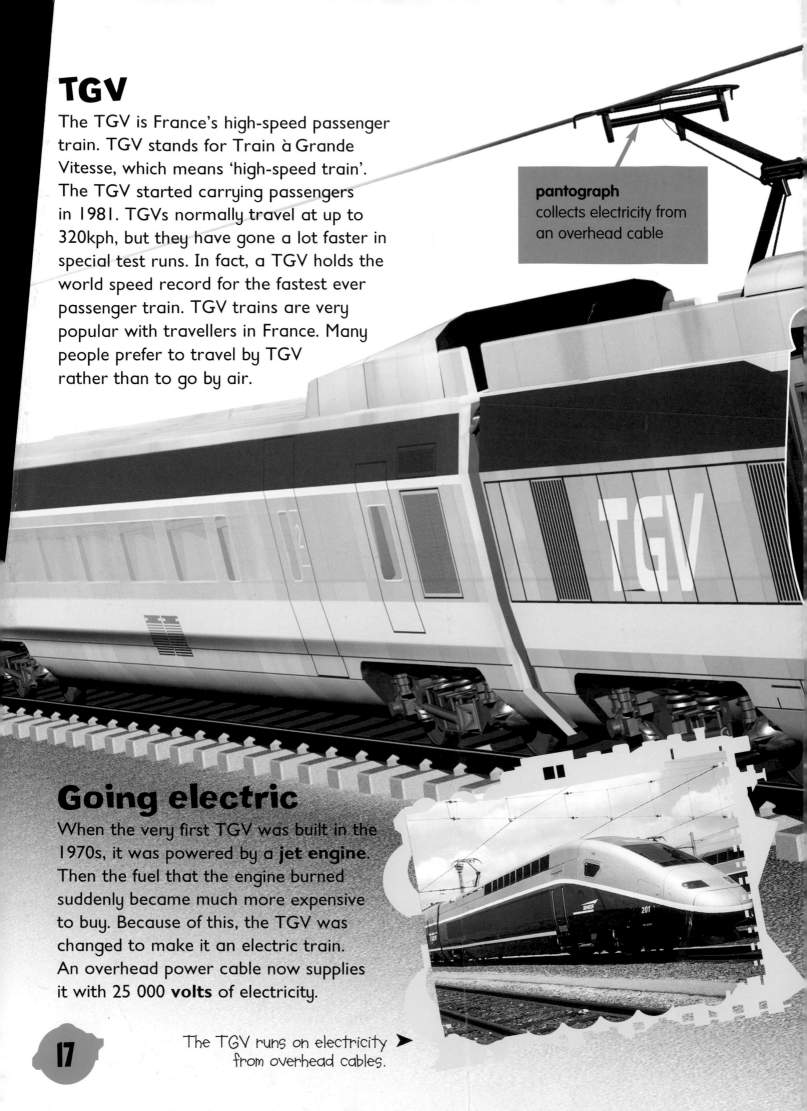

TGV

The TGV is France's high-speed passenger train. TGV stands for Train à Grande Vitesse, which means 'high-speed train'. The TGV started carrying passengers in 1981. TGVs normally travel at up to 320kph, but they have gone a lot faster in special test runs. In fact, a TGV holds the world speed record for the fastest ever passenger train. TGV trains are very popular with travellers in France. Many people prefer to travel by TGV rather than to go by air.

pantograph
collects electricity from an overhead cable

Going electric

When the very first TGV was built in the 1970s, it was powered by a **jet engine**. Then the fuel that the engine burned suddenly became much more expensive to buy. Because of this, the TGV was changed to make it an electric train. An overhead power cable now supplies it with 25 000 **volts** of electricity.

The TGV runs on electricity ➤ from overhead cables.

HIGH SPEED

High-speed trains can carry passengers at more than 200kph! Most of them are powered by electricity from wires hanging above the track. Because the train does not have big, heavy tanks of fuel, it can go faster. The shape of a high-speed train is important. The Japanese Shinkansen, the French TGV and the German ICE high-speed trains are designed to go very fast. They all have a sloping front and a smooth body to help them to slip through the air.

streamlined body

The Japanese Shinkansen ▲ train was called the **Bullet Train** when it was first seen, because of its shape and speed.

FACT!
Japanese Shinkansen trains stop automatically if they are shaken by an earthquake!

Acela Express

The fastest train in the USA is the Acela Express. It has been running the 640km between the US capital city, Washington DC, and Boston since 2000. On the fastest part of the track, it reaches 240kph.

◄ Acela Express trains have four passenger carriages between two locomotives.

ICE-COOL TRAIN

ICE stands for Inter-City Express. The ICE trains are high-speed trains made in Germany. They started running in 1991. The latest ICE trains carry passengers at up to 300kph. In tests, they have gone faster than 400kph – nearly four times faster than cars in the fast lane of a motorway!

▲ ICE trains run at top speed on their own special lines. They run at normal speeds on ordinary lines.

STOP AND GO

The movements of trains are usually controlled by signals beside the track. However, the TGV goes so fast that the driver would not have time to see signals flashing past outside. Instead, signal information is sent along the tracks. It is picked up by the train and the driver sees the signals on his instrument panel.

Traffic signals are sent straight into the driver's cab. ▲

automatic coupler connects the power car to other vehicles, if necessary

Power cars

Each TGV train has two locomotives, which are also called **power cars**. There is one at the front of the train and one at the back. They are packed full of electronic equipment, including a transformer. The transformer changes the electric current from the overhead power cable into the right form of electricity to run the train's electric motors.

▼ A TGV train has two power cars, with eight or ten carriages in-between them.

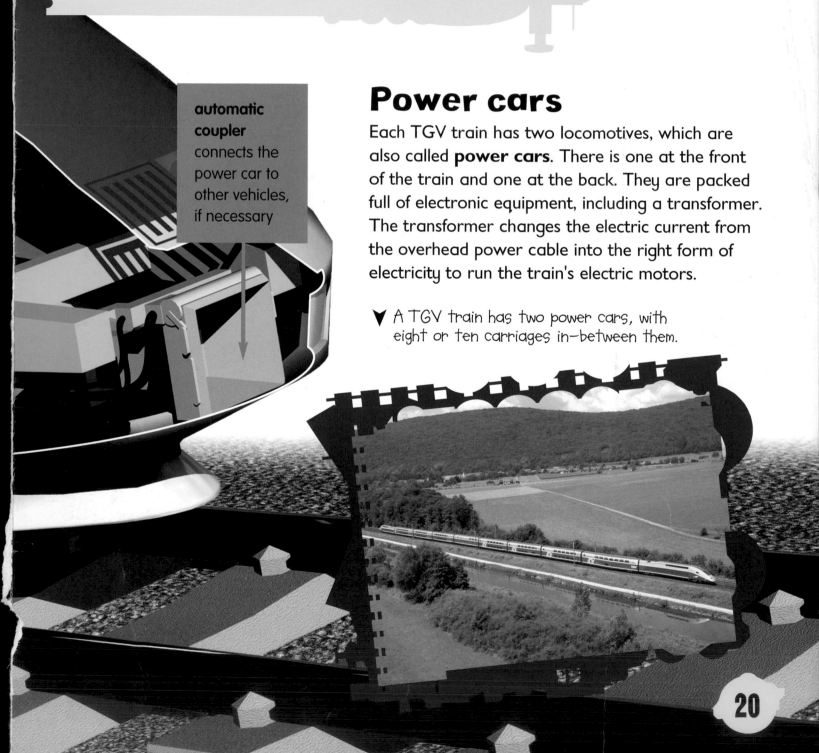

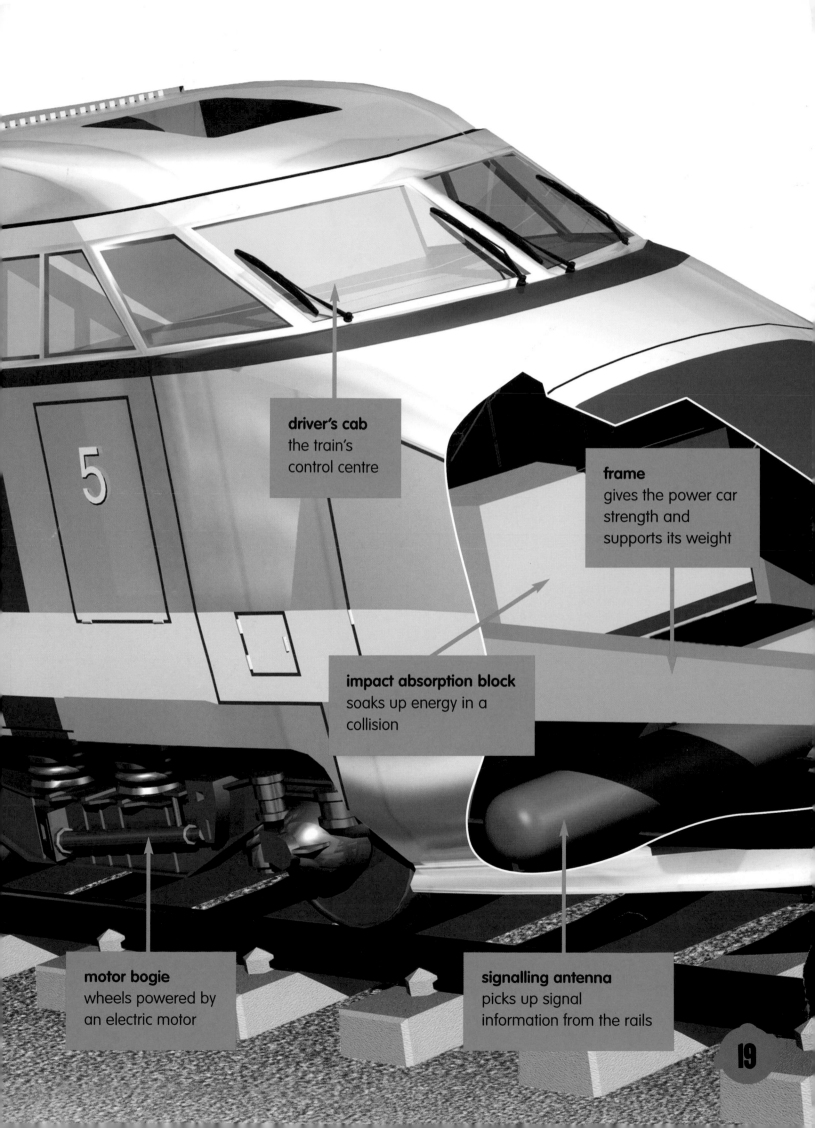

driver's cab
the train's
control centre

frame
gives the power car
strength and
supports its weight

impact absorption block
soaks up energy in a
collision

motor bogie
wheels powered by
an electric motor

signalling antenna
picks up signal
information from the rails

TUNNEL SHUTTLES

Eurostar trains are very unusual because they run under the sea! The English Channel is the sea between the south of England and the rest of Europe. Eurostar trains travel through the Channel Tunnel, which is made up of two tunnels dug through the rock beneath the sea. These electric trains are powered by 25 000 volts of electricity from an overhead power cable. A train goes through the tunnel every four minutes, travelling between London, in England, Lille, in France and Brussels, in Belgium.

FACT!

The freight locomotives that speed through the Channel Tunnel are the most powerful in the world.

Tunnel freight

A different type of train is used to carry vehicles, rather than just people, through the Channel Tunnel. The locomotives for these trains are more powerful than 40 family cars! Two locomotives pull a train weighing as much as 2400 tonnes at speeds of up to 140kph! Cars, coaches and vans are carried inside enclosed wagons. Trucks travel in different, open-sided wagons.

▲ Cars drive straight from the platform into rail wagons for their journey through the Tunnel.

TRAFFIC CONTROL

The people who control trains in the Channel Tunnel sit in front of a giant display board. This has a map of the tunnels that shows the positions of all the trains. There is an identical control room at each end of the tunnel. If one has a problem, the other can take over immediately.

▲ Channel Tunnel controllers always know exactly where every single train is, and what the signals are showing.

COMMUTER TRAINS

Commuter trains take large numbers of people from their homes into the cities where they work. These local trains are designed to carry as many passengers as possible. Some commuter trains are pulled by locomotives. Many others do not need a locomotive, either because their carriages have their own built-in diesel engines or because they have electric motors underneath the floor. Commuter trains can usually be driven from either end. This means that they can go back the way they came without having to turn the whole train around.

Local trains that have built-in motors instead of a locomotive are called multiple units.

upper deck

DOUBLE-DECKERS

Double-deck carriages can be used to fit more people into a train. However, they cannot be used everywhere. Some road bridges are too low to let these taller rail cars pass underneath.

▲ Double-deck carriages carry many more passengers per train.

FACT!
Japan has the world's biggest commuter rail network.

TILTING TRAINS

When trains go round bends, passengers feel as if they are being pushed sideways. If trains go too fast, things start sliding off the tables! Because of this, trains have to slow down when they go round bends. Slowing down and speeding up again afterwards wastes time and makes journeys longer. One answer is to build straighter tracks, like those used by the French TGV and the Japanese Shinkansen trains. Another answer is to build trains, such as the American Acela Express, that can tilt on bends.

Tilting trains are ➤ more comfortable for passengers at high speeds.

◄ Pendolino trains tilt automatically as the train goes round a curve in the track.

Little pendulum

In Italy, pendolino means 'little **pendulum**'. It is also the name of a type of tilting train that is very popular in Europe. It is used in Portugal, Slovenia, Finland, Germany, the Czech Republic and the United Kingdom. Several other countries plan to introduce these tilting trains in the future.

FACT!
The first tilting trains were developed in Spain in the 1930s.

MONORAILS

Most trains run on two steel rails, but **monorail** trains run on just one rail. This 'rail' is usually a concrete **beam**, which sits on towers so that the track is high above the ground. Monorail trains have two sets of wheels. One set supports the train's weight. A second set grips the beam and keeps the train upright. Most monorail trains ride on top of the rail, but there are a few that hang below the rail. Electric current for the motors comes from the rail.

FACT!
The world's first **commercial** monorail opened in Listowel, Ireland, in 1888.

▲ About 30 000 visitors to Las Vegas, USA, use the city's monorail to get around every day.

Hanging around

In the German city of Düsseldorf, the Sky-Train that links the airport and the railway station is a monorail. The cars hang underneath the rail, 23m above the ground. The rail is a hollow beam, and the train's wheels run inside it. The 2.5km journey takes about five minutes.

Düsseldorf's Sky-Train whisks passengers to and from the airport over the top of busy streets. ➤

DISNEY MONORAILS

Monorails have carried visitors around Walt Disney resorts since 1959. The first one opened in Disneyland, in California, USA. The trains are powered by 600 volts of electricity from the rail. Each train can sense if it is getting too close to the train in front. It warns the driver, or the train brakes automatically.

▲ Disneyland's monorail trains carry 150 000 people every day.

29

FLYERS

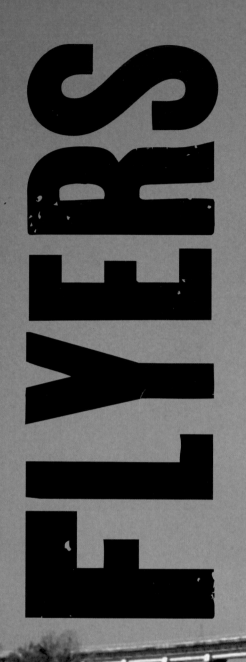

A new type of train actually flies above its track! It is called a maglev. Maglev is short for 'magnetic **levitation**'. The train rises up in the air by **magnetism**. There are powerful magnets in the train and also in the specially built track, or guideway. Magnetic forces between the train and the track lift the train up above the track and move it along. Maglevs can go twice as fast as normal trains.

The Transrapid maglev runs on a track ➤ that is raised above the ground.

FACT!

The US space agency NASA has looked into using a maglev track to launch spacecraft.

Transrapid

The first maglev for passengers runs between the city of Shanghai, in China, and Shanghai's new international airport. This maglev is known as the Transrapid. Regular passenger services began in 2004, with the train reaching a top speed of 430kph. In tests, Transrapid maglevs have gone faster than 500kph.

▲ Japan's sleek, futuristic MLX01 maglev is the fastest in the world.

FUTURE FLYERS

An experimental maglev in Japan has reached 581kph on a test track with passengers on board. The MLX01 is an advanced maglev for the future. It uses special magnets called superconducting magnets. These magnets are made super-efficient and extra-powerful by cooling them so they are many times colder than ice!

ROLLER COASTERS

A roller coaster is one of the most exciting rail vehicles you can ride in. Most roller coasters work by towing a line of carriages up a steep hill, and then releasing them. **Gravity** pulls the cars down the other side of the hill and around the rest of the track. The latest roller coasters do not rely on gravity alone. The cars are launched along the track. This makes them go faster for an even more exciting ride!

Staying on track

Roller-coaster carriages do not sit on top of their rails like railway carriages. Instead, they have wheels above, below and outside the rails, which grip the rails. The carriages cannot fall off, even when they go fast around tight turns or even turn upside-down.

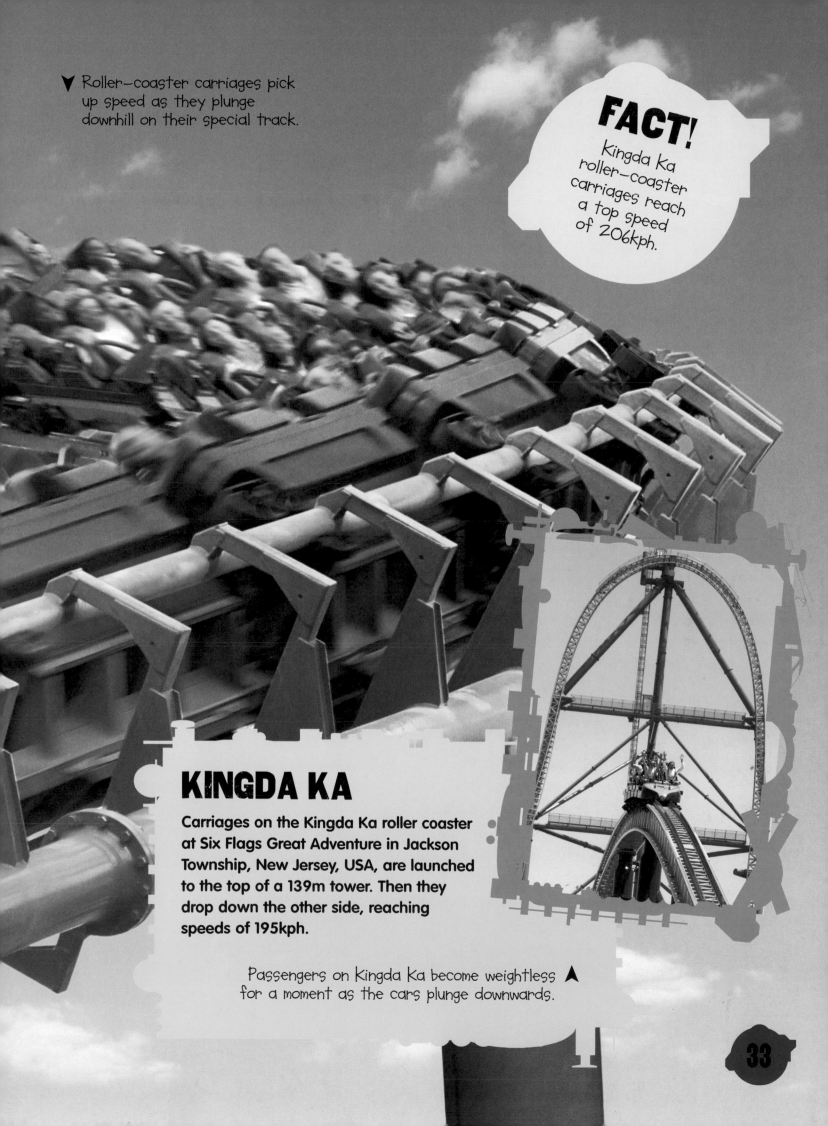

▼ Roller-coaster carriages pick up speed as they plunge downhill on their special track.

KINGDA KA

Carriages on the Kingda Ka roller coaster at Six Flags Great Adventure in Jackson Township, New Jersey, USA, are launched to the top of a 139m tower. Then they drop down the other side, reaching speeds of 195kph.

Passengers on Kingda Ka become weightless ▲ for a moment as the cars plunge downwards.

GLOSSARY

air pollution harmful substances in the air. Burning oil or petrol in vehicle engines produces harmful substances that spread through the air

beam a long, narrow piece of wood, metal or concrete, often supported at both ends

billion one thousand million

Bullet Train a nickname for the Shinkansen high-speed train in Japan. It was given this name because of the shape and speed of the first models of these trains in the 1960s

cab the part of a locomotive or train where the driver sits

carriage a railway car for passengers

commercial run as a business

commuter a person who travels the same route to work every day, often by train or car. Commuters usually travel several miles from where they live into the towns or cities where they work

cylinder a tube-shaped part of an engine where the fuel is burned

deck a floor with passenger compartments in a train

diesel engine a type of engine in some cars, buses and trucks that burns an oil called diesel oil

environment the natural world

expand to become larger

freight goods being transported

fuel a substance burned in a vehicle's engine

fumes smelly or harmful gases

gravity the force that pulls objects towards each other because of the matter they are made of. Gravity stops everything flying off the Earth into space, and it holds the planets in their orbits around the Sun. Gravity makes it hard to go uphill and easy to go downhill

high-speed train a train that goes faster than about 200kph

jet engine a type of engine that burns fuel to produce a jet of gas. Jet engines provide the power to turn a locomotive's wheels

launch to use extra power to send off a vehicle or rocket very fast

launch pad a platform from which a rocket takes off

levitation rising up into the air

locomotive an engine that moves under its own power and pulls passenger carriages or freight wagons

magnetism the ability of a magnet to pull iron towards it

mass transit a railway for moving a large number of people across a city quickly

metro an underground railway beneath a city

miniature much smaller than normal

monorail a track with a single rail for a vehicle to move along

network railway tracks connected to each other, linking towns and cities

pendulum a weight swinging from side to side on a wire or rod

piston a drum-shaped part of an engine that fits inside a cylinder. The piston can slide in and out of the cylinder. Burning fuel in the cylinder pushes the piston out of the cylinder

pollute to add unwanted or harmful substances

power car another name for the locomotive, or pulling vehicle, of an electric train

rapid transit a railway for moving people across a city quickly

remote far away from most people

restore to bring back into good condition

roller coaster a raised railway, usually found at a theme park, with curves and steep climbs. People ride in open cars for fun and excitement

satellite a smaller object orbiting a larger one. Communications satellites orbit the Earth. They can pick up signals from one place and send them to someone in a different part of the world

streamlined a smooth, gently curving shape that moves through the air quickly and easily

streetcar a passenger vehicle running on rails along city streets

subway the name for an underground railway in the USA

tram a passenger vehicle running on rails along city streets

transponder short for transmitter-responder, a piece of equipment that sends out a coded radio signal to identify a vehicle. Aeroplanes and trains carry transponders

volt measurement of electricity

wagon a rail car for carrying freight

FIND OUT MORE

Websites

See lots of interesting railways facts, railway history and games:
http://www.trakkies.co.uk

Find out more about Japan's Shinkansen 'Bullet' trains:
http://web-jpn.org/kidsweb/techno/shinkansen/index.html

Download plans for making paper models of the French TGV high-speed train:
http://www.railfaneurope.net/tgv/papermodels.html

Discover the history of trains in Canada from the stories of people who were there:
http://www.collectionscanada.ca/2/32/index-e.html

INDEX

Acela Express 21, 26
air pollution 4, 6, 34
automatic coupler 20
automatic trains 8

Baikonur Cosmodrome 11
beams 28, 29, 34
bendy cars 7
Bullet Train 16, 34

cab 15, 19, 34
carriages 4, 7, 10, 32–33, 34
Channel Tunnel 22–23
commuters 24–25, 34
containers 13
cylinders 15, 34

decks 25, 34
diesel engines 8, 12, 14, 24, 34
Disney resorts 29
double-deck trains 25
driverless trains 8

electric motors 6, 8, 9, 14, 16, 17, 19, 20, 22, 24, 28, 29
environment 4, 6, 34
Eurostar trains 22–23

freight 5, 12–13, 22, 34
fuel 5, 17, 34
fumes 8, 34

gravity 32, 34

high-speed trains 4, 5, 16–21, 34

ICE (Inter-City Express) 16, 21
impact absorption block 19

jet engines 17, 34

Kingda Ka 33

launch 32, 34
launch pad 10, 11, 34
levitation 30, 34
light rail 6–7
locomotives 5, 10, 12, 20, 22, 23, 24, 34
Los Angeles Metro Blue Line 6

maglevs 30–31
magnetism 30, 31, 34
mass transit 8, 34
metros 8, 9, 34
miniature trains 15, 34
MLX01 31
monorails 28–29, 34
motor bogie 19
multiple units 24

NASA 30
network 9, 25, 34
New York City Subway 9

Orient Express 10

pantograph 17
Paris Metro 8
Pendolino trains 26
pendulum 26, 34
petrol engines 8
pistons 15, 35
pollute 6, 35
power cable 18, 20, 22
power cars 18, 20, 35

rapid transit 8, 35
remote areas 13, 35
restore 14, 35
rockets 10, 11
roller coasters 32–33, 35

satellites 13, 35
Shinkansen train 16, 26
shipping containers 13
shuttle trains 22–23
signals 20, 23
signalling antenna 19
Sky-Train 29
speed records 14, 17
steam engines 14–15
streamlined 16, 35
streetcars 6, 35
subways 8, 9, 35
superconducting magnets 31

telescopes 10
TGV 16, 17–20, 26
tilting trains 26, 27
trams 6, 35
Transrapid 30, 31
Trans-Siberian Express 10, 11
transformers 18, 20
transponders 13, 35
Transrapid 30, 31
Trevithick, Richard 5

underground railways 8–9

volts 17, 22, 29, 35

wagons 5, 23, 35